Make & Take Sequencing Fun

Reproducible Sequencing Cards to Develop
Oral Language, Listening, and Pre-Reading Skills

by
Sherrill B. Flora

illustrated by
Janet Armbrust

Publisher
Key Education Publishing Company, LLC
Minneapolis, Minnesota

CONGRATULATIONS ON YOUR PURCHASE OF A KEY EDUCATION PRODUCT!

The editors at Key Education are former teachers who bring experience, enthusiasm, and quality to each and every product. Thousands of teachers have looked to the staff at Key Education for new and innovative resources to make their work more enjoyable and rewarding. We are committed to developing and publishing educational materials that will assist teachers in building a strong and developmentally appropriate curriculum for young children.

PLAN FOR GREAT TEACHING EXPERIENCES WHEN YOU USE EDUCATIONAL MATERIALS FROM KEY EDUCATION PUBLISHING COMPANY, LLC

Credits
Author: Sherrill B. Flora
Inside Illustrations: Janet Armbrust
Cover Illustration: Mary Eden
Creative Director: Mary Claire
Editor: George C. Flora

Key Education welcomes manuscripts and product ideas from teachers. For a copy of our submission guidelines, please send a self-addressed, stamped envelope to:
Key Education Publishing Company, LLC
Acquisitions Department
9601 Newton Avenue South
Minneapolis, Minnesota 55431

ISBN:1-933052-03-1
Make & Take Sequencing Fun
Copright © 2005 by Key Education Publishing Company, LLC
Minneapolis, Minnesota 55431

Contents

Introduction

Make & Take Sequencing Fun will quickly become a valued and frequently referenced early childhood classroom resource. This book is filled with beautifully illustrated sequencing cards that were designed to assist children with three-scene, four-scene, six-scene, and eight-scene sequencing activities. Simply copy the pages needed for the children and allow them to color, cut out, and use the cards for the following activities:

- telling and re-telling events, songs, stories, and rhymes;
- questioning and predicting outcomes;
- developing an understanding of the concepts of beginning, middle, and end;
- encouraging oral language skills;
- assisting with left to right orientation;
- enhancing the development of visual discrimination skills; and
- developing effective listening skills.

The wide variety of sequencing concepts will keep the children engaged and challenged. At first, simply present the children with three-scene events that they are familiar with, such as eating, baking, or playing in the sand. As the children become more proficient at sequencing three-scene events, the teacher can follow the natural progression and use sequences that become more visually and logically complex.

Make & Take Sequencing Fun can also be used for enhancing listening skills. For example, the teacher can read one of the stories; retell an event; say a rhyme; or have the children sing a song; and then have the children place the cards in the proper sequence according to what they have just heard. The children will delight in being able to bring home the cards and share what they have learned with their parents!

Sequencing Scenes

The reproducible sequencing cards for three-scene, four-scene, and six-scene events can be found on pages 6 through 24. Copy the page for each child. Have the children color the pictures and cut them out along the dotted lines. Specific directions for each event can be found on that specific page.

Listening Activities and Story Narratives for the 6-Scene Sequences
(Reproducible cards found on pages 20–24.)

Baking a Cake! *(Event found on page 20.)*

Have the children prepare the sequencing cards. As you read the following events to the children, have them arrange the cards in the proper sequence of the story.

"Juan is a hungry little boy. He decided that he was going to bake a cake all by himself. **(a)** He first had to find everything that he was going to need and put it all on the kitchen counter. **(b)** He then put all the ingredients in a big bowl and stirred the batter. **(c)** When the batter was ready, Juan poured it into a cake pan. **(d)** He put the cake pan in the oven and waited. **(e)** When the cake was done, he spread the frosting on the cake! **(f)** Juan finished his cake and was very proud of his beautiful cake!"

What a Great Artist! *(Event found on page 21.)*

Have the children prepare the sequencing cards. As you read the following events to the children, have them arrange the cards in the proper sequence of the story.

"Emily wanted to be a painter. **(a)** She stood at her easel with her paints, but couldn't decide what she wanted to paint. **(b)** She started painting the sky. **(c)** She kept working and added birds and land. **(d)** When Emily added trees, her painting looked almost done. **(e)** Look, Emily is standing by her easel with her finished work. **(f)** Her parents were so proud of Emily's painting that they had it framed and hung it on a wall—just like a real artist."

Flying High! *(Event found on page 22.)*

Have the children prepare the sequencing cards. As you read the following events to the children, have them arrange the cards in the proper sequence of the story.

"Jonathan had always been a brave boy, but today he was going to be the bravest he had ever been. **(a)** He walked over to a huge hot air balloon. After taking many flying lessons, he was ready for his first solo flight. **(b)** Jonathan climbed into the basket. **(c)** Once inside the basket, he untied the ropes. **(d)** Soon the hot air balloon began to rise. **(e)** The balloon floated high in the air and you could see Jonathan waving good-bye. **(f)** Before long, Jonathan could hardly be seen. But don't worry, he will get home safely."

Eating Out! *(Event found on page 23.)*

Have the children prepare the sequencing cards. As you read the following events to the children, have them arrange the cards in the proper sequence of the story.

"For a special birthday treat Joe took Kassie to her favorite restaurant for dinner. **(a)** They walked into the restaurant and found an empty table. **(b)** They sat down and began to read the menu. **(c)** Soon, a waitress came over to the table and took their order. **(d)** Joe and Kassie did not wait long before the waitress was back with their food. **(e)** Oh. . . the food was delicious! Kassie and Joe enjoyed a wonderful meal. **(f)** After they were done eating, they paid their bill and left to go home. What a great birthday dinner!"

Let's Go Swimming! *(Event found on page 24.)*

Have the children prepare the sequencing cards. As you read the following events to the children, have them arrange the cards in the proper sequence of the story.

"Kayla was an excellent swimmer, but she wasn't so sure about the pool slide. She decided that she should be brave enough to try the slide. **(a)** At first she just stood at the bottom of the ladder. It looked safe. **(b)** She then slowly began climbing up the ladder. **(c)** Pretty soon she was sitting on the top of the slide. It feels pretty high up! **(d)** Kayla gave herself a small push and began to slide down. **(e)** Before she knew it, she was at the bottom of the slide . . . and then SPLASH into the water! **(f)** Standing in the water, she waved to her friends and said, "that wasn't so scary after all!"

Yummy Ice Cream Cone! - 3 Scene Sequence

Directions: Copy the page for each child. Cut off the directions. Have the children color, cut along the dotted lines, and arrange the cards in proper sequence.

Listening activity: Read the following events to the children. Have them arrange the cards as you read the story. **(a)** "Once there was a little boy who had a very large ice cream cone. **(b)** He was so hungry that he licked and licked the cone. **(c)** Soon the cone was gone. Some of the ice cream was in his tummy, and some of the ice cream was all over his shirt!"

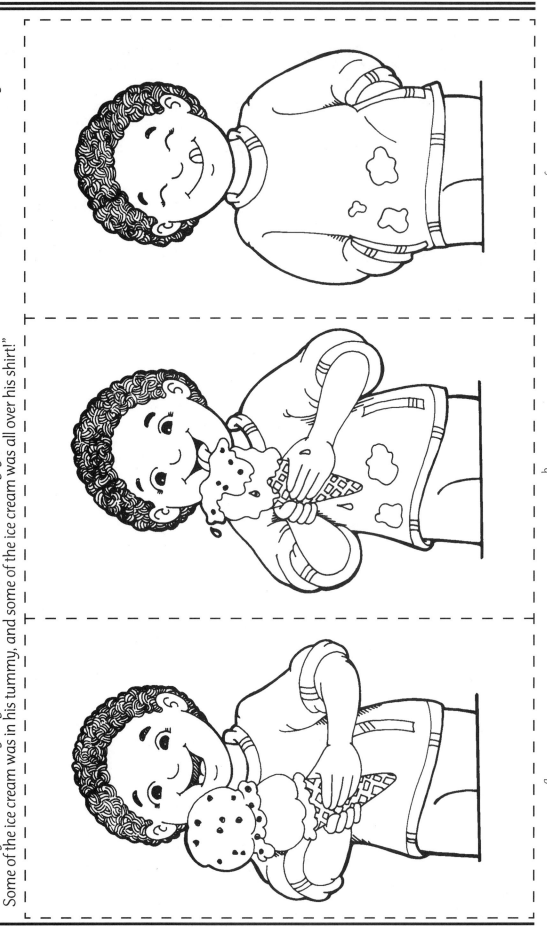

a

b

c

What a Cracked Egg! - 3 Scene Sequence

Directions: Copy the page for each child. Cut off the directions. Have the children color, cut along the dotted lines, and arrange the cards in proper sequence.

Listening activity: Read the following events to the children. Have them arrange the cards as you read the story. **(a)** "Once upon a time, there was a huge egg laying in the grass. Suddenly, a noise could be heard coming from the egg. **(b)** The egg started cracking and two little eyes peeked through the crack. **(c)** Look! A baby alligator!"

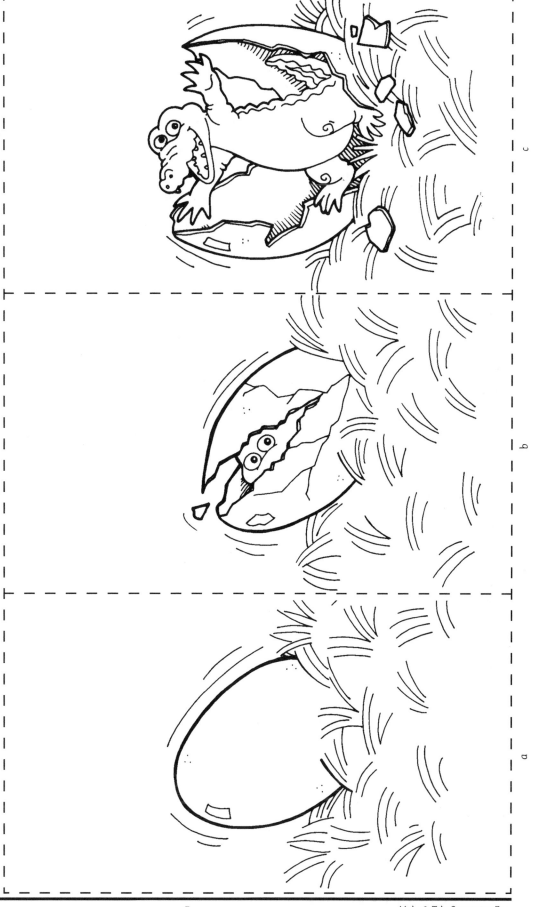

c

b

a

7

Birds in a Tree! – 3 Scene Sequence

Directions: Copy the page for each child. Cut off the directions. Have the children color, cut along the dotted lines, and arrange the cards in proper sequence.

Listening activity: Read the following events to the children. Have them arrange the cards as you read the story. **(a)** "At the top of the tree lived two little birds. It was a hot day so the birds decided that they wanted to go swimming. **(b)** They flew down and landed in the birdbath. **(c)** They splashed and splashed all afternoon!"

Playing in a Sandbox! - 3 Scene Sequence

Directions: Copy the page for each child. Cut off the directions. Have the children color, cut along the dotted lines, and arrange the cards in proper sequence.

Listening activity: Read the following events to the children. Have them arrange the cards as you read the story. **(a)** "One day, a little girl named Jasmine, took her pail and shovel and sat in her sandbox. **(b)** She started to build something very big and very beautiful. **(c)** Jasmine built a huge sand castle!"

a

b

c

Look at that Frog Grow! - 3 Scene Sequence

Directions: Copy the page for each child. Cut off the directions. Have the children color, cut along the dotted lines, and arrange the cards in proper sequence.

Listening activity: Read the following events to the children. Have them arrange the cards as you read the story. **(a)** "Look at all the tiny eggs floating in the pond. **(b)** Look! the eggs are changing. They look like little fish, but they are really tadpoles. **(c)** The tadpoles have finished growing! Look at all the frogs!"

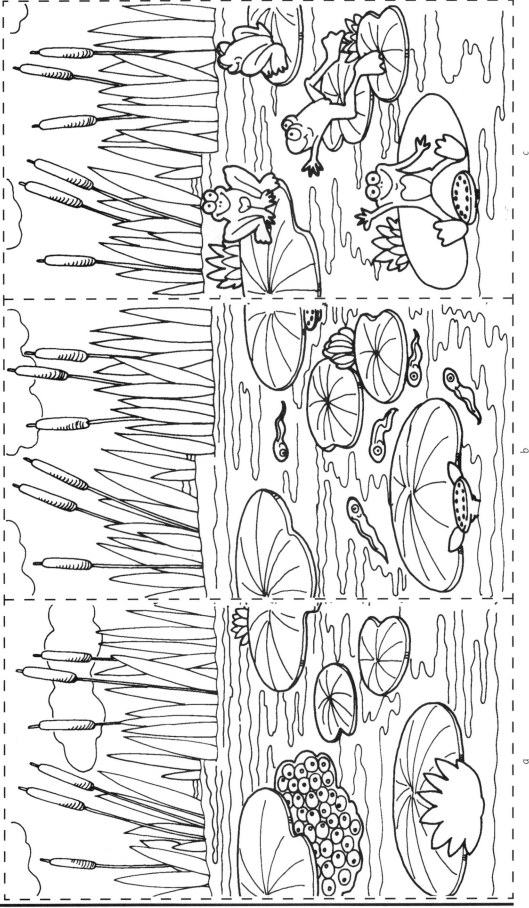

a   b   c

Oh, I'm Thirsty! - 3 Scene Sequence

Directions: Copy the page for each child. Cut off the directions. Have the children color, cut along the dotted lines, and arrange the cards in proper sequence.

Listening activity: Read the following events to the children. Have them arrange the cards as you read the story. **(a)** "This little girl has had a busy day and she is thirsty. **(b)** She picks up the pitcher and pours herself a tall glass of lemonade. **(c)** She drinks the lemonade and oh, it tasted so good!"

a

b

c

Great Big Balloon! - 4 Scene Sequence

Directions: Copy the page for each child. Cut off the directions. Have the children color, cut along the dotted lines, and arrange the cards in proper sequence.

Listening activity: Read the following events to the children. Have them arrange the cards as you read the story. **(a)** "Ted got a new balloon at a birthday party. **(b)** He started blowing it up. **(c)** He blew and blew and blew! **(d)** Oh no! It popped!"

a

b

c

d

Stringing Beads! - 4 Scene Sequence

Directions: Copy the page for each child. Cut off the directions. Have the children color, cut along the dotted lines, and arrange the cards in proper sequence.

Listening activity: Read the following events to the children. Have them arrange the cards as you read the story. **(a)** "This little girl's name is Maria. She wants to string beads. She picks up the string and a bead. **(b)** She adds several beads. **(c)** She has added more and more beads. **(d)** She made a beautiful necklace and is wearing it."

I Love Pie! - 4 Scene Sequence

Directions: Copy the page for each child. Cut off the directions. Have the children color, cut along the dotted lines, and arrange the cards in proper sequence.

Listening activity: Read the following events to the children. Have them arrange the cards as you read the story. **(a)** "Oh my, Tim and Jenn have found a pie! **(b)** Tim says, 'I will cut the pie for us.' **(c)** Jenn says, 'I will serve the pie.' **(d)** And then they both giggled and said, 'we will both eat the pie! Yum!' "

a

b

c

d

14

Let's Build a Snowman! - 4 Scene Sequence

Directions: Copy the page for each child. Cut off the directions. Have the children color, cut along the dotted lines, and arrange the cards in proper sequence.

Listening activity: Read the following events to the children. Have them arrange the cards as you read the story. **(a)** "It's a beautiful winter day. Let's play in the snow and build a snowman. Let's first make a large snowball for the body. **(b)** Then we will make a middle-sized snowball. **(c)** Now we will make a snowball for his head. **(d)** Finally, we will give him a face."

What a Dirty Dog! - 4 Scene Sequence

Directions: Copy the page for each child. Cut off the directions. Have the children color, cut along the dotted lines, and arrange the cards in proper sequence.

Listening activity: Read the following events to the children. Have them arrange the cards as you read the story. **(a)** "Zach loves his dog, but that dog sure does like to get dirty! **(b)** Zach's dog is sad, but he still has to get in the water. **(c)** Zach takes the soap and begins to get his dog good and clean! **(d)** Oh no! Now Zach is the one who is all wet!"

An Apple a Day! - 4 Scene Sequence

Directions: Copy the page for each child. Cut off the directions. Have the children color, cut along the dotted lines, and arrange the cards in proper sequence.

Listening activity: Read the following events to the children. Have them arrange the cards as you read the story. **(a)** "A little worm crawled on top of a big, red, juicy apple. **(b)** He thought, maybe I should have one little taste of the apple. **(c)** Before long, that little worm had eaten half of that big, red, juicy apple. **(d)** Suddenly, the little worm wasn't so little anymore, and the apple was all gone!"

a

b

c

d

Bedtime! - 4 Scene Sequence

Directions: Copy the page for each child. Cut off the directions. Have the children color, cut along the dotted lines, and arrange the cards in proper sequence.

Listening activity: Read the following events to the children. Have them arrange the cards as you read the story. **(a)** "It had been a very long day and Jacob was tired. He put on his pajamas. **(b)** Then he turned down the blankets. **(c)** Jacob climbed into bed! **(d)** And before long, Jacob fell sound asleep."

Let's Write a Letter! - 4 Scene Sequence

Directions: Copy the page for each child. Cut off the directions. Have the children color, cut along the dotted lines, and arrange the cards in proper sequence.

Listening activity: Read the following events to the children. Have them arrange the cards as you read the story. **(a)** "Marie's grandmother lives out of town. Marie misses her grandmother. She decides to write her grandmother a letter. Marie sits down and writes the letter. **(b)** Then she puts the letter in an envelope. **(c)** She places a stamp on the envelope. **(d)** And finally, she walks down the street and places her letter in the mailbox."

Baking a Cake! - 6 Scene Sequence

Directions: Copy the page for each child. Cut off the directions. Have the children color, cut along the dotted lines, and arrange the cards in proper sequence.

Listening activity: The narrative for these sequencing cards is found on page 5. Have the children place the cards in proper sequence as they listen to the narrative.

What a Great Artist! - 6 Scene Sequence

Directions: Copy the page for each child. Cut off the directions. Have the children color, cut along the dotted lines, and arrange the cards in proper sequence.

Listening activity: The narrative for these sequencing cards is found on page 5. Have the children place the cards in proper sequence as they listen to the narrative.

Flying High! - 6 Scene Sequence

Directions: Copy the page for each child. Cut off the directions. Have the children color, cut along the dotted lines, and arrange the cards in proper sequence.

Listening activity: The narrative for these sequencing cards is found on page 5. Have the children place the cards in proper sequence as they listen to the narrative.

Eating Out! - 6-Scene Sequence

Directions: Copy the page for each child. Cut off the directions. Have the children color, cut along the dotted lines, and arrange the cards in proper sequence.

Listening activity: The narrative for these sequencing cards is found on page 5. Have the children place the cards in proper sequence as they listen to the narrative.

Let's Go Swimming! - 6-Scene Sequence

Directions: Copy the page for each child. Cut off the directions. Have the children color, cut along the dotted lines, and arrange the cards in proper sequence.

Listening activity: The narrative for these sequencing cards is found on page 5. Have the children place the cards in proper sequence as they listen to the narrative.

Nursery Rhyme Sequencing

The reproducible sequencing cards for the nursery rhymes can be found on pages 26 through 35. Copy the page or pages for each child. Have the children color the pictures and cut them out along the dotted lines. Specific directions for each rhyme can be found on that specific page.

Little Miss Muffet
(Sequencing cards found on page 28.)

(a) Little Miss Muffet sat on a tuffet,
Eating her curds and whey.
(b) Along came a spider,
(c) And sat down beside her,
(d) And frightened Miss Muffet away!

Humpty Dumpty
(Sequencing cards found on page 29.)

(a) Humpty Dumpty sat on a wall,
(b) Humpty Dumpty had a great fall.
(c) All the King's horses and all the King's men,
(d) Couldn't put Humpty together again.

Wee Willie Winkie
(Sequencing cards found on page 30.)

(a) Wee Willie Winkie runs through the town.
(b) Upstairs and downstairs in his nightgown.
(c) Rapping at the windows, crying at the locks.
(d) Are the children all in bed – for now it's 8:00.

Hey Diddle Diddle
(Sequencing cards found on page 31.)

(a) Hey Diddle, Diddle, the cat and the fiddle,
(b) The cow jumped over the moon.
(c) The little dog laughed to see such sport,
(d) And the dish ran away with the spoon.

Mary, Mary Quite Contrary
(Sequencing cards found on page 32.)

(a) Mary, Mary quite contrary,
(b) How does your garden grow?
(c) With silver bells and cockle shells,
(d) And pretty maids all in a row.

There Was an Old Woman
(Sequencing cards found on page 33.)

(a) There was an old woman who lived in a shoe.
(b) She had so many children she didn't know what to do.
(c) So she gave them a hug and a warm piece of bread.
(d) And gently tucked them all into bed.

Little Jack Horner
(Sequencing cards found on page 34.)

(a) Little Jack Horner sat in a corner,
(b) Eating his Christmas pie.
(c) He put in his thumb,
(d) And pulled out a plum,
And said, "What a good boy am I!"

There Was a Crooked Man
(Sequencing cards found on page 35.)

(a) There was a crooked man,
And he walked a crooked mile.
(b) He found a crooked six-pence against a crooked stile.
(c) He bought a crooked cat,
Which caught a crooked mouse.
(d) And they all lived together in a crooked little house.

Cackle, Cackle, Mother Goose! – Nursery Rhyme

Directions: Copy the page for each child. Cut off the directions. Have the children color, cut along the dotted lines, and arrange the cards in proper sequence.

Listening activity: Read the following nursery rhyme to the children. Have them arrange the cards as you read the rhyme.
(a) "Cackle, cackle Mother Goose. **(b)** Have you any feathers loose? **(c)** Truly I have pretty fellow. Quite enough to fill a pillow."

Hickory Dickory Dock – Nursery Rhyme

Directions: Copy the page for each child. Cut off the directions. Have the children color, cut along the dotted lines, and arrange the cards in proper sequence.

Listening activity: Read the following nursery rhyme to the children. Have them arrange the cards as you read the rhyme. **(a)** "Hickory, dickory dock. The mouse ran up the clock. **(b)** The clock struck one. **(c)** The mouse ran down. Hickory, dickory dock."

Little Miss Muffet — Nursery Rhyme

Directions: Copy the page for each child. Cut off the directions. Have the children color, cut along the dotted lines, and arrange the cards in proper sequence.

Listening activity: The nursery rhyme for these sequencing cards is found on page 25. Have the children place the cards in the proper sequence as they listen to the nursery rhyme.

Humpty Dumpty – Nursery Rhyme

Directions: Copy the page for each child. Cut off the directions. Have the children color, cut along the dotted lines, and arrange the cards in proper sequence.

Listening activity: The nursery rhyme for these sequencing cards is found on page 25. Have the children place the cards in the proper sequence as they listen to the nursery rhyme.

Wee Willie Winkie – Nursery Rhyme

Directions: Copy the page for each child. Cut off the directions. Have the children color, cut along the dotted lines, and arrange the cards in proper sequence.

Listening activity: The nursery rhyme for these sequencing cards is found on page 25. Have the children place the cards in the proper sequence as they listen to the nursery rhyme.

Hey Diddle Diddle – Nursery Rhyme

Directions: Copy the page for each child. Cut off the directions. Have the children color, cut along the dotted lines, and arrange the cards in proper sequence.

Listening activity: The nursery rhyme for these sequencing cards is found on page 25. Have the children place the cards in the proper sequence as they listen to the nursery rhyme.

Mary, Mary Quite Contrary - Nursery Rhyme

Directions: Copy the page for each child. Cut off the directions. Have the children color, cut along the dotted lines, and arrange the cards in proper sequence.

Listening activity: The nursery rhyme for these sequencing cards is found on page 25. Have the children place the cards in the proper sequence as they listen to the nursery rhyme.

a

b

c

d

There Was an Old Woman - Nursery Rhyme

Directions: Copy the page for each child. Cut off the directions. Have the children color, cut along the dotted lines, and arrange the cards in proper sequence.

Listening activity: The nursery rhyme for these sequencing cards is found on page 25. Have the children place the cards in the proper sequence as they listen to the nursery rhyme.

Little Jack Horner – Nursery Rhyme

Directions: Copy the page for each child. Cut off the directions. Have the children color, cut along the dotted lines, and arrange the cards in proper sequence.

Listening activity: The nursery rhyme for these sequencing cards is found on page 25. Have the children place the cards in the proper sequence as they listen to the nursery rhyme.

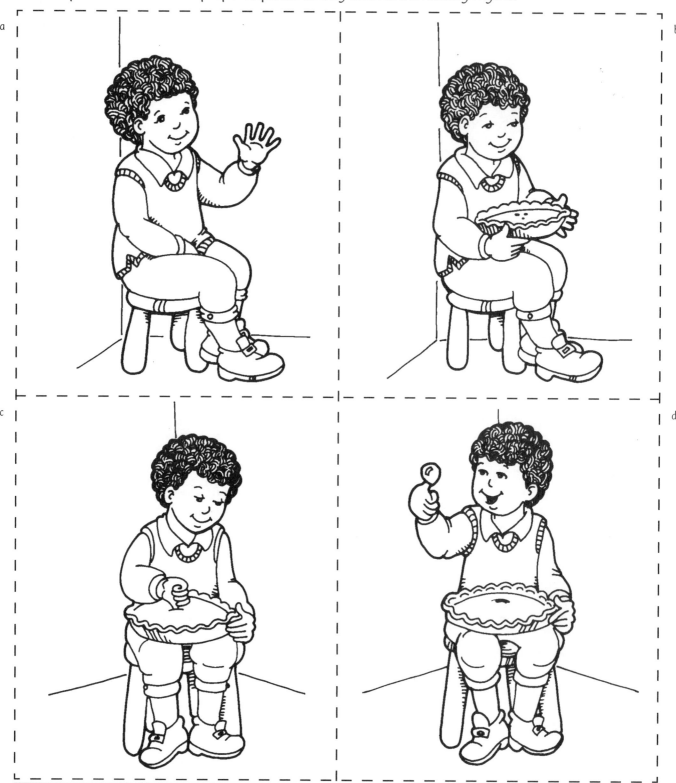

There was a Crooked Man – Nursery Rhyme

Directions: Copy the page for each child. Cut off the directions. Have the children color, cut along the dotted lines, and arrange the cards in proper sequence.

Listening activity: The nursery rhyme for these sequencing cards is found on page 25. Have the children place the cards in the proper sequence as they listen to the nursery rhyme.

Children's Song Sequencing

The reproducible sequencing cards and the words to the children's songs can be found on pages 37 through 44. Copy the page or pages for each child. Have the children color the pictures and cut them out along the dotted lines. Specific directions for each song can be found on that specific page.

The Wheels on the Bus

(Sequencing cards found on page 43–44.)

(a) The wheels on the bus go round and round, round and round, round and round.
The wheels on the bus go round and round, all through the town.

(b) The horn on the bus goes beep, beep, beep – beep, beep, beep – beep, beep, beep.
The horn on the bus goes beep, beep, beep, all through the town.

(c) The wipers on the bus go swish, swish, swish – swish, swish, swish – swish, swish, swish.
The wipers on the bus go swish, swish, swish, all through the town.

(d) The driver on the bus says, "move on back, move on back, move on back."
The driver on the bus says, "move on back," all through the town.

(e) The children on the bus go up and down, up and down, up and down.
The children on the bus go up and down, all through the town.

(f) The babies on the bus go, "waa, waa, waa – waa, waa, waa – waa, waa, waa."
The babies on the bus go, "waa, waa, waa," all through the town.

(g) The parents on the bus go, "shh, shh, shh – shh, shh, shh – shh, shh, shh.
The parents on the bus go, "shh, shh, shh," all through the town.

Jack and Jill – Children's Song

Directions: Copy the page for each child. Cut off the directions. Have the children color, cut along the dotted lines, and arrange the cards in proper sequence.

Listening activity: Read or sing the following nursery rhyme song to the children. Have them arrange the cards as you read or sing the rhyme. **(a)** "Jack and Jill went up the hill to fetch a pail of water. **(b)** Jack fell down and broke his crown. **(c)** And Jill came tumbling after."

Mary Had a Little Lamb – Children's Song

Directions: Copy the page for each child. Cut off the directions. Have the children color, cut along the dotted lines, and arrange the cards in proper sequence.

Listening activity: Read or sing the following nursery rhyme song to the children. Have them arrange the cards as you read or sing the rhyme. **(a)** "Mary had a little lamb, little lamb, little lamb. Mary had a little lamb whose fleece was white as snow. **(b)** It followed her to school one day, school one day, school one day. It followed her to school one day which was against the rules. **(c)** It made the children laugh and play, laugh and play, laugh and play. It made the children laugh and play to see a lamb at school."

Baa, Baa Black Sheep
Children's Song

Directions: Copy this page and page 40 for each child. Cut off the directions. Have the children color, cut along the dotted lines, and arrange the cards in proper sequence.

Listening activity: Read or sing the following nursery rhyme song to the children. Have them arrange the cards as you read or sing the rhyme.

Baa Baa Black Sheep

(a) Baa baa black sheep, have you any wool?

(b) Yes sir, yes sir, three bags full.

(c) One for my master.

(d) One for my dame.

(e) One for the little boy who lives down the lane.

(f) Baa baa black sheep, have you any wool?

Yes sir, yes sir, three bags full.

c

d

e

f

Sing a Song of Six Pence
Children's Song

Directions: Copy this page and page 42 for each child. Cut off the directions. Have the children color, cut along the dotted lines, and arrange the cards in proper sequence.

Listening activity: Read or sing the following nursery rhyme song to the children. Have them arrange the cards as you read or sing the rhyme.

Sing a Song of Six Pence

(a) Sing a song of six pence, a pocketful of rye.
Four and twenty blackbirds baked in a pie.
When the pie was opened the birds began to sing.
(b) Now wasn't that a dainty dish to set before the king.
(c) The king was in the counting house, counting all the money.
(d) The queen was in the parlor, eating bread and honey.
(e) The maid was in the garden, hanging out the clothes.
(f) Along came a blackbird and snipped at her nose.

a

b

c

d

e

f

Wheels on the Bus!
Children's Song

Directions: Copy this page and page 44 for each child. Cut off the directions. Have the children color, cut along the dotted lines, and arrange the cards in proper sequence.

Listening activity: Sing, "Wheels on the Bus" with the children. The lyrics are found on page 36. Have the children arrange the cards as you read or sing the song.

a

b

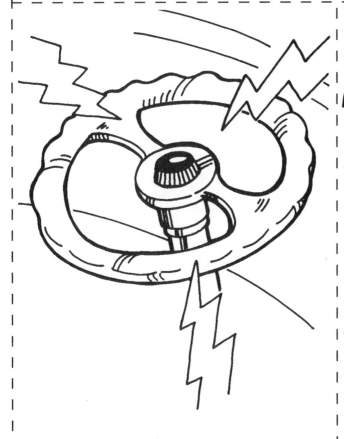

c

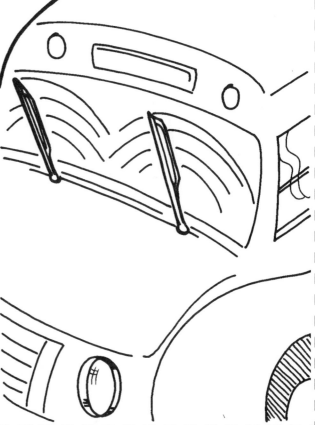

d

e

f

g

Classic Children's Stories Sequencing

The stories and reproducible sequencing cards for six classic children's stories can be found on pages 46 through 64. Copy the appropriate page or pages for each child. Have the children color the pictures and cut them out along the dotted lines.

Goldilocks & the Three Bears
The Story

Once upon a time, in a far away forest, lived the kind and friendly family of the Three Bears. Papa Bear was very big and had a very loud growl. Mama Bear was middle-sized, with a soft and loving growl. And Baby Bear was the smallest. His growl sounded more like a squeak!

In a small village, on the other side of the forest, lived another family of three. A good father, a caring mother, and a little girl who often found herself in a great deal of trouble. She was named Goldilocks because of her long blond curls. This is the story of how the two families met.

(a) One morning, back in the forest, Mama Bear had prepared some delicious porridge for breakfast. It smelled wonderful, but was too hot for the bears to eat. The bears decided to go on a walk while they waited for their porridge to cool.

Meanwhile, back in the village, Goldilocks asked her parents if she could go outside and play. Her parents said "yes," as long as she stayed in her own yard. Goldilocks did not think her parents would notice if she was gone for just a few minutes. She ran off down the path and into the forest to pick flowers. Her parents had told her many times that she was not allowed to wander into the forest, but, she went anyway . . .

(b) It wasn't long before Goldilocks realized that she was lost! She should have listened to her parents. A small cottage came into view. Goldilocks said, "I will knock on the cottage door and ask for help." She knocked on the door, but no one was home. She turned the doorknob and discovered that the door was unlocked! She opened the door and went in!

The aroma inside the house was wonderful! It made Goldilocks feel very hungry. She saw three bowls of porridge on the kitchen table. She picked up the spoon for the very large bowl, tasted the porridge, and exclaimed, "Oh my!" "This is far too hot!" She picked up the next spoon, tasted the porridge in the middle-sized bowl, and said, "Oh dear! This is way too cold." **(c)** Finally, Goldilocks picked up the tiny spoon, tasted the porridge in the baby-sized bowl, and said, "This is just right!" Goldilocks gobbled up all of Baby Bear's porridge!

Curious, Goldilocks wandered into the family room and saw three chairs. She jumped up on the largest chair and nearly fell off. It was much too big. Then Goldilocks climbed up on the middle-sized rocking chair and discovered that it rocked way too much. **(d)** Finally, Goldilocks sat down on the littlest chair and it broke!

Feeling tired. Goldilocks went upstairs and found the bedroom. She climbed up onto the largest bed, but it was way too hard. She then climbed up onto the middle-sized bed and it was way too soft. **(e)** Finally, Goldilocks jumped up onto the littlest bed and fell sound asleep.

When the bears came home they found their front door open! They were worried that someone was in the house, so they tiptoed into their cottage! **(f)** Papa Bear spotted his bowl of porridge and growled, in a very loud growl, "Someone has been eating my porridge!" Mama Bear said in a very gentle growl, "Someone has been eating my porridge!" And Baby Bear squeaked a small growl, and said, "Someone has been eating my porridge and that someone ATE IT ALL UP!"

The bears walked quietly into the family room where Papa Bear said with a big growl, "Someone has been sitting on my chair!" Mama Bear said in her soft growl, "Someone has been sitting in my chair!" **(g)** And last, Baby Bear squeaked a baby growl and cried, "Someone has been sitting in my chair and BROKE IT!"

Finally, the bears went upstairs to their bedroom. What they saw was a huge surprise! Papa Bear growled in a very loud growl, "Someone has been sleeping in my bed!" Mama Bear said in a soft growl, "Someone has been sleeping in my bed!" And, Baby Bear squeaked the loudest growl he could, and said, "Someone has been sleeping in my bed, AND THERE SHE IS!" **(h)** At that moment, Goldilocks jumped up, screamed, ran down stairs, and flew out the front door— where she bumped right into her frantic parents!

Goldilocks' parents were so happy to have found her, but they were also upset that Goldilocks had left her own yard to wander in the forest. They were also not pleased that she had gone uninvited into the Bear's cottage. Goldilocks' parents marched her back to the front door and had her apologize to the Bear family. Of course, the Bears forgave her and asked Goldilocks' family to stay for breakfast and enjoy some of Mama Bear's delicious porridge!

a

b

c

d

e

f

g

h

The Three Pigs — The Story

(a) Once upon a time, there were three pigs who were all brothers. The three pigs had always lived together in the same little house. One day, they all sat down and decided that their little house was simply too small for all three of them. They all decided that they should each build their own little house. So each of the three pigs set out with a wheelbarrow and tools so they could each build their own new house.

(b) The first pig, named Peter, was the laziest of all the brothers. Peter decided that it would be faster to build a small house made of straw. Straw was easy to find and very light to carry. It would be fast to build a house of straw. So, that's what he did!

(c) The second pig, named Paul, was a better worker than Peter, but he still wanted to finish his house quickly. Paul decided that he would use sticks to build his house. Sticks were also very easy to find. In a very short time, Paul could build a house of sticks! So, that's what he did!

(d) The third pig, named Patrick, was the hardest worker of the three pigs. He decided to build his house out of brick. Bricks were difficult to find and heavy to carry, but Patrick knew that brick would make the strongest and safest house. So, that's what he did! Before long, all three of the brothers were settled in their new homes.

However, someone new has moved to the neighborhood—a wolf! No one was very happy about this because wolves were known to be very bad neighbors. Each of the brothers locked their doors and hoped that the wolf would simply choose to leave the neighborhood.

(e) Before long, the wolf snuck over to Peter's house of straw. The wolf knocked, listened, and then roared, "Let me in, let me in, or I'll huff and I'll puff, and I'll blow your house in!" Peter squealed, "Not by the hair of my chinny, chin, chin!" "Well then," growled the wolf, "I'll huff and I'll puff, and I'll blow your house in!" So, that's what he did! And just when the straw house was falling down, Peter escaped out the back window and ran all the way to his brother Paul's house.

The two little pigs, Peter and Paul, shivered with fear in the corner of the stick house. **(f)** When all of a sudden the wolf appeared, knocked at the door, and then roared, "Let me in, let me in, or I'll huff and I'll puff, and I'll blow your house in!" Peter and Paul squealed, "Not by the hair of our chinny, chin, chins!" "Well then," growled the wolf, "I'll huff and I'll puff, and I'll blow your house in!" So, that's what he did! And just when the stick house was falling down, Peter and Paul escaped out the back window and ran all the way to their brother Patrick's house.

The two little pigs, Peter and Paul, shivered with fear in the corner of the brick house, but Patrick was not afraid. He knew his house was strong and safe! **(g)** All of a sudden the wolf appeared, knocked at the door, and then roared, "Let me in, let me in, or I'll huff and I'll puff, and I'll blow your house in!" Peter, Paul, and Patrick all squealed, "Not by the hair of our chinny, chin, chins!" "Well then," growled the wolf, "I'll huff and I'll puff, and I'll blow your house in!" So, that's what he tried to do, but the little brick house stood strong. The wolf tried again and roared, "Let me in, let me in, or I'll huff and I'll puff, and I'll blow your house in!" As hard as the wolf tried, the little brick house stood strong.

Soon the wolf decided in order to get those little pigs he would have to climb up onto the roof and then climb down the chimney. The smart little pigs heard the wolf on the roof. They quickly built a fire in the fireplace. **(h)** Just as the wolf slid down and almost reached the fire, the flames slapped the wolf's bottom and sent him flying back up the chimney—never to be seen or heard from again!

The little pigs learned a couple of lessons that day. First, Peter and Paul learned that the easy way is not always the best way. Patrick's house was better because he built his house with the strongest building materials. Secondly, the little pigs learned that it was much more fun to live together! So, that's what they did!

a

b

c

d

e

f

g

h

51

The Big Lion and the Little Mouse – The Story

Once upon a time, in a forest far away, lived many, many animals. Some of the animals were very big and some of the animals were very small. This is a story about one of the biggest animals and one of the smallest animals.

(a) The first animal we are going to hear about is one of the biggest and is called, "the King of the forest" — the lion! The lion loved to spend his days hunting and eating, and eating and hunting! He lived alone and believed that he did not need any friends. He didn't need friends because all he wanted to do was hunt and eat, and eat and hunt.

(b) In this same forest lived a very small mouse. Since he was one of the smallest animals in the entire forest, he had to be very careful. The mouse never knew which of the bigger animals might want to eat him. The mouse managed to stay safe by hiding in the blades of grass.

(c) One day when the mouse was busy looking for seeds and grains to eat, he accidently stumbled over a big, brown, furry something. "Oh my," thought the mouse, "This was so soft. What could I have fallen over?" As the mouse studied the big, brown, furry something, he looked up a little and noticed that the big, brown, furry something was attached to a face with large dark eyes, a big nose, and huge teeth!

(d) Suddenly, the big, brown, furry paw grabbed the little mouse by the tail and held him up in the air. "Well now, what do I have here?" roared the lion. Squeaking, the little mouse cried, "Please, don't eat me!"

"And why not?" drooled the lion. The little mouse certainly looked mighty tasty!

Pleading, the little mouse said, "I just know that we could be good friends and good friends help each other! Today you can help me by letting me go, and the next time we meet, I can help you!"

The lion laughed and laughed and laughed! "How could a small mouse like yourself ever help a big lion like me?" roared the lion.

"You never know," said the mouse. "Size does not matter when you are friends. I know that someday my friendship could really help you."

(e) The lion admired the mouse's courage, so he let the mouse go. The lion was also not very hungry at the moment. The mouse scampered off, feeling very grateful that the lion had found some kindness in his heart.

About a week later, the mouse was once again busy looking for seeds and grains. Suddenly, he heard a horrible roar. Something very large is in trouble! The mouse scampered through the grass and listened as the roar became louder and louder! Soon the mouse spotted the lion. Hunters had been in the forest and had set a trap for the lion. **(f)** There lay the lion, caught and tangled in the hunter's thick knotted ropes.

"Please be quiet, lion," squeaked the mouse. "I will help you get out of this mess."

"Oh little mouse" cried the lion. "How can you help me?"

"I know what to do," exclaimed the mouse. **(g)** I can chew through the ropes and set you free before the hunters return. The little mouse chewed so fast that the lion was free in just a few minutes.

(h) Now, if you ever visit this forest, you might just see a very small mouse riding on the back of a very big lion—who just happens to be his very best friend.

a

b

c

d

Make & Take Sequencing Fun

Make & Take Sequencing Fun

The Three Billy Goats Gruff
The Story

(a) Once upon a time, in a beautiful land of thick green grass and rolling hills, lived three brother billy goats, named Gruff. The three billy goats were easy to tell apart because they were all different sizes. The youngest Billy Goat Gruff was very small, the second Billy Goat Gruff was medium-sized, and the oldest Billy Goat Gruff was very large.

The three Billy Goats Gruff also made different sounds. **(b)** The littlest Billy Goat Gruff had a tiny voice and made tiny hoof "tripping" sounds. It always sounded like this, "trip, trip, trip."

(c) The middle-sized Billy Goat Gruff had a medium-sized voice and made medium-sized hoof "trotting" sounds. It always sounded like this, "trot, trot, trot."

(d) The largest Billy Goat Gruff had a loud and large-sized voice and made loud and large-sized hoof "tromping" sounds. It always sounded like this, "tromp tromp, tromp."

One day as the three brothers were on the beautiful rolling hills, grazing on the thick green grass, they looked over at the grass on the other side of the bridge. Somehow the grass on the other side of the bridge looked thicker and greener than their grass. All three of the Billy Goats Gruff decided they wanted to eat the grass on the other side of the bridge.

To get to the other grass, the three Billy Goats Gruff had to walk over the bridge. This was not an easy thing to do because an ugly troll with hairy feet and sharp teeth lived under the bridge. He did not like anyone walking over his bridge.

(e) The littlest Billy Goat Gruff decided to go first. He began "tripping" over the bridge. The troll heard the little "trip, trip, trip," jumped up on the bridge and yelled, "Who is tripping over my bridge? I am going to eat you!"

"It is I, the littlest Billy Goat Gruff. Please don't eat me. I am much too little. Wait for my brother. He is bigger than I am and will fill you up much more than I would," cried the little Billy Goat Gruff.

"Oh, alright! You can walk over my bridge. I will hide and wait for your bigger brother," growled the ugly troll.

(f) Then came the middle-sized Billy Goat Gruff. He began "trotting" over the bridge. The troll heard the middle-sized "trot, trot, trot," jumped up on the bridge and yelled, "Who is trotting over my bridge? I am going to eat you!"

"It is I, the middle-sized Billy Goat Gruff. Please don't eat me. I am not very large. Wait for my brother. He is much bigger than I am, and will fill you up much more than I would," explained the middle-sized Billy Goat Gruff.

"Oh, alright! You can walk over my bridge. I will hide and wait for your bigger brother," growled the ugly troll.

(g) Finally, the largest Billy Goat Gruff began "tromping" over the bridge. The troll heard the loud and large "tromp, tromp, tromp," jumped up on the bridge and yelled, "Who is tromping over my bridge? I am going to eat you!"

"It is I, the largest Billy Goat Gruff and you will not eat me." In the next moment, the loud and large Billy Goat Gruff picked up the troll with his huge horns and threw him over the bridge and into the river. The mean and ugly troll was never seen again!

(h) After that, the largest Billy Goat Gruff tromped over the bridge to join his two brothers. The three Billy Goats Gruff grazed on the thick green grass on the other side of the bridge. Their biggest surprise was that the grass tasted the same on both sides of the bridge!

a

b

c

d

e

f

g

h

The Gingerbread Man
The Story

Once upon a time, on a nice farm, lived an old man and an old woman. They were very happy on the farm. The old man took care of all the farm animals, and the old woman loved to bake.

(a) Today began the same way as most everyday. The old man woke up and fed the animals, and the old woman began her baking. Today the old woman decided to bake a gingerbread man—complete with raisin eyes, a cherry chip nose, and a licorice mouth. She placed him in the oven to bake and set the timer.

(b) When the timer buzzed, the old woman took the gingerbread man out of the oven, and to her surprise, the gingerbread man was sitting up on the cookie sheet! He looked at the old woman and sang, "Run, run, as fast as you can. You can't catch me, I'm the gingerbread man." The old woman ran out the door chasing after the gingerbread man and yelling, "Stop! Stop, I'll catch you—I can. You can't run away from me, gingerbread man!"

(c) The gingerbread man kept running until he bumped right into the old man who was milking the cow. The old man tripped over his milking bucket, fell to the ground, and yelled, "Stop! Stop, I'll catch you—I can. You can't run away from me, gingerbread man!"

"You don't say," said the gingerbread man. "Run, run, as fast as you can. You can't catch me, I'm the gingerbread man. I ran away from the old woman and I can run away from you, I can."

(d) The gingerbread man ran and ran until he tripped over the dog. The dog growled a hungry growl, licked his chops and said, "Stop! Stop, I'll catch you—I can. You can't run away from me, gingerbread man!"

"You don't say," said the gingerbread man. "Run, run, as fast as you can. You can't catch me, I'm the gingerbread man. I ran away from the old woman, and the old man, and I can run away from you, I can."

So, the parade of runners kept growing! **(e)** The gingerbread man led the way, followed closely by the old woman, the old man, and now the dog. The gingerbread man was running around the farm pond when he nearly crashed into the duck. The duck flapped his wings and squawked, "Stop! Stop! I'll catch you—I can. You can't run away from me, gingerbread man!"

"You don't say," said the gingerbread man. "Run, run, as fast as you can. You can't catch me, I'm the gingerbread man. I ran away from the old woman, the old man, the dog, and I can run away from you, I can." So off they all flew, with the gingerbread man leading the way!

Then the gingerbread man ran into the forest. **(f)** He tripped over a log and bumped into the fox. Now this was a crafty fox and he knew he could not catch the running gingerbread man. So, the fox did not yell, "Stop! Stop, I'll catch you—I can. You can't run away from me, gingerbread man!" Instead the fox said, "Hide, hide, gingerbread man. I'll help you escape, I can! I can!"

Well, the gingerbread man stopped running and said, "I'm so tired! I ran away from the old woman, the old man, the dog, the duck, and I can't run anymore. I don't think I can."

"Come with me," said the fox, "and I'll protect you—I can!" **(g)** The crafty fox led the gingerbread man into his cave and picked him up to put him in his cookie jar, and later gobbled him up! *(After all, he was a cookie!)*

(h) Meanwhile, the old woman, the old man, the dog, and the duck are still running and looking for the gingerbread man! You can hear them yelling, "Stop! Stop! We'll catch you—we can. You can't run away from us, gingerbread man!"

a

b

c

d

e

f

g

h

The Little Red Hen — The Story

(a) Once upon a time, on a beautiful old farm, lived a little red hen, a cow, a pig, a dog, and all the little chicks. All the animals were very good friends and usually liked to help each other.

(b) Today the little red hen strutted out of her hen house and clucked, "Oh, I am soooo hungry, and my grain box is empty. What should I do?"

The little dog heard the hen and barked, "Oh, I am soooo hungry, and my dog dish is empty."

Next came the pink little pig who oinked, "Oh, I am soooo hungry, and my food pan is empty."

And finally, the cow mooed, "Oh, I am soooo hungry, and my food troft is empty."

The little red hen declared, "We should all work together and bake some bread. Doesn't that sound wonderful?" All the animals agreed that some fresh warm bread straight out of the oven sounded great!

(c) "Who will help me?" asked the little red hen. "First we have to go into the field and gather the wheat."

"I am so sorry," barked the dog, "but I am soooo tired. I need a nap."

"I am so sorry," oinked the pig, "but I am soooo tired. I need a nap."

"I am so sorry," mooed the cow, "but I am soooo tired. I need a nap."

(d) "Oh, very well, I will do it myself," clucked the little red hen. And so she did! She ran off into the field and gathered all the wheat. **(e)** When she returned with the wheat, she said to her friends, "I am back with the wheat. Now, who will help me grind the wheat into flour?"

"I am so sorry," barked the dog, "but I am still soooo tired. I need a longer nap!"

"I am so sorry," oinked the pig, "but I am still soooo tired. I need a longer nap!"

"I am so sorry," mooed the cow, "but I am still soooo tired. I need a longer nap!"

(f) "Oh, very well, I will do it myself," clucked the little red hen. And so she did! She worked so hard to grind the wheat into flour. **(g)** "Now, who will help me turn the flour into bread dough?"

"I am so sorry," barked the dog, "but I am still soooo tired. Wake me in an hour!"

"I am so sorry," oinked the pig, "but I am still soooo tired. Wake me in an hour!"

"I am so sorry," mooed the cow, "but I am still soooo tired. Wake me in an hour!"

(h) "Oh, very well, I will do it myself," clucked the little red hen. And so she did! She worked so hard turning the flour into bread dough! **(i)** "Now, who will help me bake the dough?"

"I am so sorry, but my nap is not over yet," barked the dog.

"I am so sorry, but my nap is not over yet," oinked the pig.

"I am so sorry, but my nap is not over yet," mooed the cow.

(j) "Oh, very well, I will do it myself," clucked the little red hen. And so she did! She poured the dough in a bread pan, put the pan in the oven, and waited for the bread to finish baking. Soon, wonderful smells of warm fresh bread were coming from the kitchen. **(k)** "Now, who will help me eat the bread?"

"I will!" barked the dog.

"I will!" oinked the pig.

"I will!" mooed the cow.

(l) "Oh, no," clucked the little red hen. "I went to the field and gathered the wheat. Then I ground the wheat into flour. Then I turned the flour into bread dough and, finally, I baked the dough that turned into the bread. All of you were too tired to help! Now I am going to eat the bread!" And that is what she did!

61 *Make & Take Sequencing Fun*

a

b

c

d

e

f

g

h

63